In memory of
Sathya
(T V Sathyamurthy)
1929-1998;
and for
D J Enright

AUTHOR'S NOTE

These poems attempt to distil, from wide comparative reading and reflection, what I found most significant in a two-year study of the *Hitlerzeit* (Hitler era): on Hitler, his accomplices and those whose lives they affected.

Formally, the poems are meant to compose a virtual narrative, a "documentary poem" or poetic history, as comprehensive in scope as I could manage. Literally manage, for I am conscious of unfilled gaps—as, for example, in my failure to complete poems on two brave and honourable leaders of the German *Widerstand* (Resistance). Claus Stauffenberg and Adam von Trott zu Solz.

Often, I felt a dispassionate, almost factual treatment was demanded. Considering the rival claims of "truth" and "pleasure" Coleridge concluded, "a poem of any length neither can be, nor ought to be, all poetry." Wary of embellishing the truth on the most "unpleasant" of subjects (a phrase from the German historian Golo Mann I've adopted for my title), I can only hope that where, in D J Enright's ironic phrase "the crude vulgarity of meaning" predominates, the poetry is still, in Coleridge's words, "in keeping": that is, poetic *enough* . . .

About half the poems are footnoted, to set them in contexts with which it cannot be assumed many readers will be familiar: I hope, therefore, they will seem helpful rather than obtrusive, in Samuel Johnson's phrase, "a necessary evil."

Hitler's dictatorship . . . showed what we are capable of.

IAN KERSHAW
Hitler, 1998

CONTENTS

I

THE FÜHRER

That is the greatest thing about him,
That he is not only our leader and great hero,
But himself upright, firm and simple,
In him rests the root of our world,
And his soul touches the stars
And yet he remains a man like you and me.
                    BALDUR VON SCHIRACH
        in J Fishman, *Long Knives and Short Memories*, 1986

Long voluntary subjection under individual Führers
and usurpers is in prospect. People no longer
believe in principles but will, periodically, probably
believe in saviours . . .
                    JACOB BURCKHARDT (1882)

As long as one believes that the evil man wears horns,
one will not discover an evil man.
                    ERICH FROMM
        The Anatomy of Human Destructiveness, 1973

What's in a Name?

Heil Schicklgruber!* was no fit salute
for customs official (or tyrant)
so years before he was born
his upwardly mobile father Alois
sired the Führer's hard name.

*Alois Schicklgruber changed his name to
 Alois Hitler in 1876. Adolf was born in 1889.

Landscapist Manqué I

(Student 1908)

That he was no despicable artist
his *Skizzenbuch* attests,
kept by him to his broken end,
mute witness to the life unlived:
watercolours of escape and awe,
remote mountain and forest, glimpsed spire,
a roiling Turneresque seascape,
firs fretted with sunset fire—
but attempting the Academy in Vienna,
deficiency of human "heads" failed him . . .

He might have become, had they let him through,
a routine misanthropic academician
vision tunnelled beyond the human,
patronized by bourgeois Gentile and Jew.

3

Freud Meets Young Hitler

(An Imaginary Dialogue in Vienna's Golden Autumn)

"Frankly, young man, you suffer
        from messianic delusion
        and morbid regression
potentially harmful to you and others,
unless you learn to sublimate your anger;
happiness, remember, is not promised us—
but new life may spring from discontent.

Your obsession with death stems in part
from your untimely loss of a loved mother,
to which and your father's brutality
your aggressive feelings are not unrelated.
I must also recognize societal pressures,
for you tread this city's streets in poverty
daily affronted by paraded wealth,
brooding upon a scapegoat. I am troubled,
I must admit, though not myself orthodox,
by your fixed antipathy to Jews:
most needful is that you discover Eros—

and where but in yourself, if art is your métier?
Though the Academy rejects you, draw strength
from that, and attempt here, in Vienna,
the creative heights of our civilization:
art compensates; if it seldom enriches,
it may console. Devote yourself to that,
Man's supreme expression."
                "I don't give a fart
for your decadent Yid's notions of art!"

Such was the gauche young Adolf's brief retort,
but when he later returned,* armed with resistless

4

monologue, Freud had moved to a distant address.

*Adolf's "return" was his triumphant entry into Vienna
to mark the *Anschluss*, March 1938
(see also "Reading History During the *Anschluss*").

Of Mice . . .*

How might it have moved us when he relates
that, in his obscure and struggling time,
he shared crusts with the mice in his room—
whose fellowship in poverty touched him—
       had we met such an anecdote
       in a Life of martyred hero or saint.

*In *Mein Kampf*.

Meldegänger

(Dispatch Runner)

See Adi running, running,
the brave unimportant corporal
through the Great losing War's
stupendous clamour:
          crouching,
taciturn, in slimy fetid dug-outs
or in the mess, brooding outside
the beery filth of sex;

within his sullen helmet's
inverted pot brews a vision
of transcendent command over
the spike-helmeted stiff generals
whose messages he
the destined usurper bore
towards their necessary defeat.

Jailed Autodidact

(after the failed *Bierhallputsch* 1923)

Insouciant laurel wreath upon his wall,
he made Landsberg* his university
where he read to distil confirmation
of all that he knew already—
Nietzsche, Marx, Houston Chamberlain,
reckless preachers of vital force,
prototypes of *Mein Kampf*'s
bilious messianic surety:
Nazidom's holy unread tome,
in a people's edition for newly-weds
Anti-Christ's subversive testament.

*Landsberg Am Lech, where Hitler served only nine months
of a five year sentence for treason, a leisurely interval during
which he began *Mein Kampf*.

Führer ex Machina

(1932)

It was always, ran the legend,
fair "Führer weather" when he spoke,
who arranged to drop from the sky
anywhere in Germany in a day—
his plane illumined by night
before its descent, godlike—
yet he was not from above, but level,
the providential Führer
miraculously born of the people,
to voice their shame, all
they deeply hated and feared,
the Ultimate Unknown Soldier
top hats and frock coats betrayed*—
apotheosis of the Nobodies,
a twentieth-century hero . . .

He was indeed ordinary,
with extraordinary self-belief—
proof in a land of philosophers
one could become what one wills,
Hegel's "world-historical man"
bending life beyond reason:
though Nietszchean vision foretold
and Heidegger's *mitdasein*† endorsed,
Hitler, a harder thinker,
combining fist and brain, wrote
"The strongest man is right."

* Betrayed: Hitler thrived upon attacking the "back-stabbers"
who negotiated the excessively punitive Treaty of Versailles, 1919.
His airborne electioneering campaign was called "Hitler Over Germany."

†*mitdasein*: togetherness.

7

"Rape and Murder"

(René Schickele, on Hitler's Speeches)

The crowd to him was "woman"—
whom he could never love as one
but only as fanaticized mass—
in orgiastic delirium he and they
died to their commonplace selves
and arms outthrust in acclaim
became filled with the spirit
that transcends and rose again—
One People, One Purpose, One Leader.

Yet it is said that *post coitum*
their *Führer*, the Nation's Bridegroom,
drained actor behind the scene,
relapsed to the twilight solitude
of the lice-ridden dropout,
denizen of Viennese doss houses,
cut-rate hawker of postcard art.

Work-out of the Monumental Man

Daily, before an open window,
he would tune his biceps
that he might stand for hours
in Roman salute, rigid
above the eyes-right columns
of booted, devoted automatons.

Behold the Man!

("How the people loved him!"—Hans Frank)

When you see his exposed limousine
crawl through the frenzied streets,
you are witness he was much loved:
with bravery you must admire,
knowing himself a simple target,
he stood "quietly upright"* in his car:
none had courage or certainty to shoot
at a resentful people's saviour.

* Hitler's words (*Hitler's Table Talk*, p. 453).

Autobahn

Concrete symbols of the course he set
were THE ROADS OF THE FÜHRER
whose openings, with flags and flowers,
they cheered, waved from arching bridges—
but all had eventually to detour
upon side roads where their gas ran out,
stranded among potholes and cracked asphalt.

9

Health Food

Teetotal, vegetarian, advocate
of the Roman legions' cereal diet,
he mocked all "corpse-consumers"—
though he gorged upon such fare
in atrocious metaphor . . .

Gnadentod*

Whatever he ordained or said, only
once did he sign an order to kill—
"granting" incurables elimination
by The Charitable Foundation
for Institutional Care: a design
for the senile and insane
that opened the way for licensed killing
of "degenerates"— whose means of disposal
he never chose to know or observe.

This fastidious ignorance he enjoined
upon all in his circle, among whom
discussion of their shared atrocities
was forbidden— for wives' and friends'
tranquility and to quarantine conscience.

*gnadentod: mercy death

His Loves

> Monster or clown, with that cow-lick,
> tar-brush moustache, costive
> superman stance, outthrust arm,
> how believe he inspired love,
> was gifted with charm?

To begin, Dolfy was his mother's darling
who, some claim, her early death undid.
In time, he recovered to fix desire
upon his light-hearted niece, Geli Raubal,
in clammy grasping and jealousy—
but when in '31 she shot herself
he retired to their flat in München,
for two weeks mourned his model Mädchen,
nearly, it was said, destroyed himself;
thereafter, beneath her sculpted bust,
a bowl of flowers was daily refreshed,
and none, he ordered, might utter her name.

Such, seemingly, was the one love of the gauche
provincial who, bearing dog whip and pistol,
dazzled but distanced the salons' bejewelled women.
Later, infatuated simple ones would worship
der schone Adolf, fall before him in ecstasy,
glean the very stones he trod, leave unwashed
the hand he clasped, or else enshrined the water—
       as Béranger's old peasant woman*
       treasured Napoleon's unrinsed glass—
thousands more sent letters of love, or sewed
arty swastikas into birthday slippers;
wealthy spinsters willed the Party their all.

By these unmoved, perhaps he loved only
his dogs—Prinz, Blondi, Wolf, Foxl—

11

pliant creatures of wordless devotion—
yet in this Eva Braun was nearly
their equal, though still human
and woman—so that claiming to fear
a wife's demands he would not marry
until, in belated tribute to her loyalty,
he wedded her to speechless death.

*Béranger: "Songs of the People"

Love Letters for Dolfy

He was their Hottest Lover,
"Sweet as Sugar little Wolfie";
they begged a phial of his sperm,
would kiss his precious prick and bum
(yes, so some groupies greeted him)—

And one was the Virgin Mary
alerted by a voice from above
that she would bear his son—
if ever there was Demon Lover
Mighty *Führer*, Little Adolfy was it.

For, playing the Exalted Redeemer,
pure Adolf yielded his body to none
of those thousands— while the Gestapo
judged the most persistent "Unfit to Live"
        cancelled their fantasy
        with reality's syringe.

Victor's View from the Right Bank

(June, 1940)

"Wasn't Paris beautiful?"
Enthused the *artiste manqué*
admirer of the Champs Elysées
and *meurtrier extraordinaire.*

Operation Barbarossa*

I. June 1941
Resolved to general his fears
he kicked open the dark room's door:
defying Napoleonic memory
to be undone, as he foreknew
by the soft agonizing ambush of snow.

II. November 1942
At one of his Russian War's darkening moments
the ex-corporal's glittering dining car
chanced to pause abreast of cattle wagons
crammed with his burnt-out, famished *übermenschen*[†]
returning west; shunning what their faces told
he signed to a servant to lower the blinds.

*The code name for Hitler's invasion of Russia, after the German hero
and Holy Roman Emperor Frederick I, known as Barbarossa
from the Italian for "Red Beard." Hitler's armies crossed the border
on 22 June, 1941, the date Napoleon's *Grande Armée* marched into
Russia 129 years before. "I've always hated snow" (*Table Talk,*
19 February 1942)

[†] *Ubermenschen:* supermen

Days and Nights at the Berghof*

("It was all very familial"—Speer)

Frequent, prolonged meals, banal talk,
an unswerving daily routine, the walk
down through woods to the Teahouse
admiring the panorama in phrases
all had heard him voice before—
innocently, it would bloom for him,
Alpine roses, blue gentians, azaleas,
the snow-sprinkled Unterberg above:
his dearest wish was that all might
share in nature's delight . . .
Replete with cream cakes he would doze—
only thus was his monologue stayed.

Dinner would be followed by westerns,
though later mindful of his soldiers' privations
he renounced those unGerman diversions
for Wagnerian operas and operettas,
while they sipped looted sparkling wine
from France: such was the victor's routine.

But at night, as from his bed
during sleepless hours he mused upon
the moonlit mountains above the Berghof
their pristine brightness dazzled his mind.

*Hitler's "magic" or "holy" mountain retreat in southeast Bavaria.

Landscapist Manqué II*

One cherished fantasy was to survive
the distracting business of war,
to wander in Italy, an unknown painter,
shy watercolourist of unpeopled nature:

to become that obscure, romantic figure
beret'd, knapsacked, burdened only
with collapsible easel— to raise it
alone, in an alpine meadow
or on the banks of the Arno—
unremarked by the select Super Race
strolling through his Thousand Year Reich.

* "My dearest wish would be to be able to wander about
in Italy as an unknown painter" (*Table Talk*, p. 11).

"The Heavens Proclaim the Glory of the Eternal"—AH*

He was, toady Bormann flattered,
"very religious," God's appointed,
the Aryan enemy's scourge . . .
Yet it was only a rhetoric he deployed,
with a tonguefull of righteous tags—
scavenged perhaps from Father Schwartz,
the priest he baited when a pupil at Linz,
confessing "fleshly sins" he fantasized,
asking to see corsets and bloomers
at the Abbé's maiden relative's store—
what a mischievous young Dolfy,
a harmless, bright-faced prankster
who would knock and run off,
innocent as yet of a single crime.

15

Concordat: Führer and Pontiff*

Both kept silence for dubious ends;
each obsessively cleansed his hands.

*The actual Concordat between Nazi Germany and the Vatican
was signed in 1933. In 1930, addressing Party journalists, Hitler
had said, "I lay claim to political infallibility," drawing an analogy
with the Pope. Various biographers record Hitler's cleanliness
fetish (shared with Himmler), while that of Pope Pius XII is
recorded in the memoirs of his personal physician Galeazzi-Lisi.

Child Lover

(AH: "They all belong to me")

Ribbentrop protested he couldn't believe
(though few could ever believe Ribbentrop)
his Führer had authorized Auschwitz—
for children ran into *Onkel* Dolfy's arms,
slept with his rare smile above their beds,
Pied Piper of Gas Chambers and Ovens.

Prinz Ponders

I sniff his scent when absently
he reaches down to pat my head;
I jump, fetch sticks, leap fences—
but he is seldom with me,
and mostly I lie expectant,
unknowing what he does elsewhere.

*Prinz, Hitler's favourite German Shepherd, is a central figure
in Günter Grass's Die_Hundejahre (The Dog Years, 1965).

Hitler and the Conspirators' End*

Was it indeed his sadistic diversion—
or only a titillating canard—
that he relished repeated screenings
of the conspirators' agonizing slow deaths
suspended by piano wire from meat hooks?

Some attest that, oddly fastidious,
as a carnivore shuns a slaughterhouse,
he shrank from observing the coarse epiphanies
his vengeful appetite demanded . . .

Also claimed, but harder to believe true,
is that each was dropped on a hempen rope,
fell at once unconscious and died in seconds—
that the Führer decreed so swift an end . . .

*The plot to kill Hitler on 20 July, 1944, narrowly failed. There are
 several conflicting accounts of the conspirators' execution and Hitler's
 attitude to it, none definitive (see I Kershaw, Hitler Vol. II, p. 693).

How Hitler and the Plotters
Finally Converged

Remarkably, by minutes or inches, all plots
against him failed. It was, he believed,
providential, he was saved to fulfil his ends
until, those denied, he chose his death's moment;
while his reluctant, would-be assassins—
absolving their *Führer* oath for Germany's sake—
always fearing chance would frustrate them,
sought vindication in the attempt itself:
at last, in their deaths *Führer* and plotters
converged in righteous conviction . . .

Totem

He lived by the totemic Adolf—
derived, he learned, from Noble Wolf.*
"Herr Wolf" was his pseudonym,
his HQ the wolf's lair or den
and his SS élite a ravening pack
that fed upon the "mutton-herd."
His chieftain's features were vulpine—
to the worshipping Winifred Wagner
he was familiarly Conductor Wolf.

Behind this puppetry lurked the myth
of raging Wotan and Fenrir his wolf,
of the final, absolute destruction
the *Führer* willed upon his *Volk*:
man-god of both future and past,
he blessed the People's Car at Wolfsburg,
but gave them Ragnarok at last.

* Noble Wolf: *Athal Wolf* (OG)

18

The Last Birthday Parade

20 April 1945

In his final photograph Hitler
pats the cheek of one among
his last young devotees—
bearers of his eternal *Reich*—
their faces aglow at the touch
of the appalling Pied Piper,
though he looks merely old
and strained, all venom drawn:
thus to their end the Chosen Children
worshipped the Father of Slaughter
in a hating Love's name.

Last Orders

He aimed his ultimate hate
at the "inadequates"* who failed him,
who did not therefore deserve to survive
the ruin they had made together.
All must be burnt, fragmented—
rubble and famine rule at last
over the Leader's weak betrayers
who had proved unworthy of life:
Defeat meant their craven desertion
of the Artist of Destruction.

minderwertigen

19

Mad Clown

Many, when it was over, retailed that fiction
how he gnawed carpets, foamed at the mouth,
a pretence that the ordainer of atrocities
should himself caper monstrously . . .

It was thus his indicted satraps
offered up their Miracle Man
as *Kranke Schweinehund*, sick swine—
unlike those he seduced truly insane . . .

In His Own Words*

"He who does not possess power loses the right to life."
"Cruelty impresses."
"What luck for the rulers that men cannot think."
"No nation will let its fingers be burnt twice. The trick of the Pied Piper of Hamelin catches people only once."
"I'm extraordinarily humane."
"Hatred is more powerful than love."
"The eternal mouthings about the communal spirit which brings men together of their own free will, make me smile."
"Nothing is lovelier than horticulture."
"We have seen what a people is capable of, when it is led. All possibilities exist in it, for good as well as evil."
"Mankind has grown great in eternal struggle, and only in eternal peace does it perish." (*MK*)
"Thank God, I've always avoided persecuting my enemies."
"I've a horror of people who enjoy inflicting tyranny upon others' bodies and tyranny upon others' souls."
". . . war is . . . a manifestation of life, it is even life's most potent and most characteristic expression."

20

"My discernment tells me that an end must be put to the reign of lies. It likewise tells me that the moment is not opportune."

"To achieve great things it is necessary to burn many of one's boats behind one especially those which are laden with personal prejudices. Reason alone must have the last word."

"In an hour when a national body is visibly collapsing and to all appearances is exposed to the gravest oppression, thanks to the activity of a few scoundrels, obedience and fulfilment of duty toward them amount to doctrinaire formalism, in fact pure insanity, if the refusal of obedience and 'Fulfilment of duty' would make possible the salvation of a people from its ruin." (*MK*)

*All quotations, except the first, from a speech in 1939, and those marked *MK* (*Mein Kampf*) are from Hitler's *Table Talk*.

II

EXECUTIVES   AND   EXECUTIONERS

Seeing this thing through and nevertheless
apart from certain exceptions due to human
infirmity—remaining decent, that is what has
made us hard.

HEINRICH HIMMLER

der Tod ist ein Meister aus Deutschland sein Auge is blau:
Death is a master from Germany his eyes are blue

PAUL CELAN

One of the lessons of Nazism, and indeed of all other
totalitarianism, is that a reserve of people suited to
the most abhorrent and horrible types of state are in
existence in potential, and usable when the time comes

ROBERT CONQUEST

.

Hitler's Paladin

Flying ace of the Richtofen wing,
he played the bluff, bemedalled figurehead,
the people's *mensch* who, some fantasized,
might humanize the cold excessive Führer:

"I decide who's a Jew," he boasted—
and so it was for the few he spared—
but he shrank when faced with Hitler
who pampered him as "Renaissance Man"*—

pinguid and bejewelled, stunned by morphine,
Göring swelled into the richest German,
gazed upon his pilfered, stored Rembrandts
while Dresden's† undefended treasures burned;

slumped from grace, in eastern robes, paddled fingers
in a pot of diamonds to soothe his nerves . . .

On Nuremberg's stage he strutted again,
the Lost Leader he had never been,
played his self-slain Chief's surrogate,
ended ashes‡ in a nameless ditch.

*Göring considered himself "the last Renaissance man"; the unimpressed
dubbed him *"Reichspompführer."*
†Dresden: as Head of the Luftwaffe, Göring failed in his boast to ensure the
defence of German cities against Allied air-raids.
‡although by suicide Göring escaped hanging at Nuremberg, his remains
joined those of the hanged, scattered in an unknown spot to prevent their
becoming an object of pilgrimage.

25

Stations of the Holocaust

Model railways were Göring's passion,
but his play stations could not have included
        Sobibor, Auschwitz— or Treblinka,
with its make-believe props: a moveless clock,
timetables to meaningless destinations,
banked flowers, a station master's cottage—
        for of those he knew nothing* . . .

*In July 1941 Göring, who was officially responsible for Jewish affairs,
signed a letter to Himmler (written by the latter) authorising him to bring
about a final solution (*Endlösung*) of the Jewish question. At Nuremberg
he claimed ignorance of the extermination camps.

Goebbels: His Master's Voice

1. Romantic Disciple in '26

"I turn to those who are small and pure
to offset the harsh things I must do—
for in smashing the muck and scum
I cleanse our good German life for them.
Yet for this I, who cite sublime Schiller,
who raptly stand below the organ of Bruckner
and thrill at our baroque cities' majesty,
passionate worshipper of noble old Germany,
must wade through yid-infected bourgeois filth . . .

But when I meet him, his blue eyes like stars,
and our Wolf grips my hand, all doubts
disappear: 'We incite,' he assures, 'for truth's sake.'
Then I am again the apostle, wholly believing,
transmit my certainty, He comes, He comes . . .

26

This must go on—though life could be sweet
and I often crave love, peace and rest—
until I die for, or *with* him were best,
whether that end be blissful or damned."

2. Dr Demagogue

They dubbed him *Schrumpfgermane*, Shrunk German—
puny, club-footed, aberrant from the Aryan—
yet the SA thugs of brawn and small brain
would shield their Doctor amid hurtling steins
and, injected with his hate-sharp slogans,
surge out in brown waves from incendiary halls
to convert Berlin's streets with persuasive blows.

3. His Duality*

Apt to be played upon and filled,
self-described instrument and vessel
of the man whose myth he forged,
this was the duality of Goebbels:
both dummy and ventriloquist.

*According to Speer, "one can say that he made Hitler as much as Hitler
made him" (G Sereny, *Speer*, p. 322).

"Applied Biology"

(Rudolf Hess)

To qualify as "national comrade"
it was essential to appear
clean, loyal and fitly employed.

Unworthy were: not merely
Jewish vermin, but asocial Aryans—
the crippled, the crazy, the queers,
dropouts who tramped and panhandled,
defiled scrupulous streets and squares,
degenerates lapsed from the *volk*—
and "gypsies," disturbing vagrants
of no fixed abode (albeit of
provable Aryan origin
and exemplary racial cohesion);
genetic defectives were neutered
or driven off in "whispering coaches"
to be "euthanized" discreetly . . .

> Such worthless ones
> were deleted selectively
> as biological deviants
> from the national *genus*,
> a cleansing necessary
> to distil Blood Purity.

Schutzhaft

("Protective Custody" Defined)

"Protective Custody" meant simply
that to be spared persecution
as a person arrested or suspected
you were confined in a Camp
where the Gestapo, with impunity,
and without impediment of trial,
was empowered to torture you to death:
   thus were you protected
   from any form of justice.

The Humane Himmler

This man whose favourite word was *gnadelos**
was tender towards his select killers,
understood the cost of courage to be cruel;
though rewarded by a seaside vacation,
mass slaughter was a "difficult task":
light reflected from his earnest pince nez,
Himmler reassured he bore the burden
with and for them— thus, Zyklon B,
the humane killer devised for vermin,
would ease their stressful murders.

*merciless

Visiting With Frau Potthast

Frau Potthast* invited the Bormann *kinder*
for chocolate and cake. That was nice—
but then came a special treat,
she led them to the attic to admire
her man's wonderful furniture . . .
Every part was human bone:
a pelvis for a chair's seat,
and human its legs and feet—
customized also at Dachau
were piled copies of *Mein Kampf*
bound in *rückenhaut*† . . .

Disappointed in these amazing toys,
the children rudely fled the attic
of *"Onkel"* Heinrich Himmler . . .

*Hedwig Potthast, Himmler's mistress.
† "best back skin"

The Fanatical Bormanns

Bormann, the *Führer's* Brown Eminence,
becomes flesh only in letters to his Gerda:
"most beautiful sweetheart," he wrote,
"beloved, clever, good, loyal National Socialist wife!"
Though joined in hate, it must be conceded
they were a truly loving pair, agreed
in all that mattered, beings of sun
and light menaced by Jewish darkness;
although together they made nine recruits
for the *Volk*, repressing bourgeois possessiveness,
Gerda would have him make more, with his mistress.

30

Their letters breathe familial virtue and care
for the "suffering, dying" superior *Volk*—
but stiffened by their stoic conviction
that destiny favours, not the good, but the strong;
and thus made one in both love and hate,
they wedded themselves to the Total State.

Martin, master fixer in the anteroom,
repelled with his brutal integrity
those who grasped at the "trash" of loot and medals,
selflessly ordered all that was needful
to further the *Führer's* sacred struggle—
never left his desk to see what this meant,
for he knew and discounted all on principle,
            without reservation or scruple,
            in hard, undivided fidelity.

For himself, Bormann desired nothing more,
at War's imagined end, than a "beautiful life"
of gardening retirement, his family
ever increasing: loving husband and father,
dutiful and loyal to him he served,
he died obscurely in Berlin's fall,
followed a year later by Gerda, of cancer:
of their children, strangely seven became
"Jewish Christians," despite blood and race.

Death of Reinhard Heydrich,
"The Successor"*

Tagged Nietzschean "blond beast"[†]
and "young evil god of Death"—
like the Apollo who flayed Marsyas,
for he was a gifted performer[‡] of Haydn
and Mozart—flashing fencer and sportsman,
      he seemed quintessential exemplar
      of cultivated German barbarity:

As, self-styled "father" of a stolen country,
Heydrich rode in open cold immunity,
Czech resisters bombed his limousine;
his week's dragging end in agony,
unaccompanied by mourning violins,
may seem to argue poetic justice
is no obsolete literary device . . .

Yet for his "Man with the Heart of Iron"
      Hitler exacted an exorbitant price—
      a special transport of 3000 Jews
      1400 Czechs at Brno and Prague
      and Lidice's obliteration—
there's no balance in a transaction
between evil and a struggling good.

*As many expected (and feared).
[†]Heydrich was known in the SS as "blond beast," but the phrase originates in Nietzsche's *The Genealogy of Morals* (1887) where, in Section XI, he writes presciently: "The profound and icy suspicion which the German arouses as soon as he assumes power (we see it happening again today) [Nietzsche's parenthesis, presumably alluding to the militarization of the new German Reich of the 1870s] harks back to the persistent horror with which Europe for many centuries witnessed the raging of the blond Teutonic beast . . ."
[‡]As violinist; also gifted musically, among the leading Nazis, were Frank and Funk.

32

Hans Frank's Polish "Play"

Hans Frank, Hitler's satrap-King of Poland
lived high in the castle at Cracow:
while the ghetto starved, his table groaned,
and, though with "soft, white tender hands"*
he played Chopin (whose museum he founded),
he matched his master in hoarse avowals
to make "mincemeat" of the Polish intelligentsia
and enslave the dregs for the Reich—

that he pontificated about due legal process
was less a bone thrown his puny scruples
than a ploy to assert his killing rights
against Himmler's black executioners—
and this Himmler knew, who held over him
intelligence of his insatiable lust for loot:
later, before his judges, Frank would claim
he only meant to take in protective custody
Da Vinci's *Lady with Ermine* and the *Black Madonna*
that graced his gubernatorial suite . . .

Faced with the gallows, he discovered
a sickly religiosity and, though received
by an accommodating Church, still believed
obedience to orders mitigated his crimes:
while no such manoeuvres could save him,
they better served his supporting cast—
of lawyers and bureaucrats, doctors and jurists
who, when "The play was done, all went home"
to rehearse their amnesiac new parts—
as doctors and jurists, lawyers and bureaucrats . . .

*Niklas Frank, *In the Shadow of the Reich*, 1991, p. 267. Other details are
drawn from this bitter repudiation by Frank's son. Frank, Governor-
General of "German" Poland, was hanged at Nuremberg in 1946. In
prison, he wrote a self-serving memoir, which had an approving diehard

33

Nazi and Roman Catholic readership. "The play was done" etc. is from this valedictory memoir, *Face to Face with the Gallows*.

Executing Orders

The Case of Otto Ohlendorf*

A rarely fastidious murderer,
immune to fantasies of blood and soil,
Otto Ohlendorf knew the better
yet followed the worst— but still
found ways to square his dual psyche:
   protested mass executions,
   then directed them dutifully;
   to absolve the individual
   prescribed collective shootings;
found in gassing a tidy solution
easier upon both killers and killed—
   and having discharged that task
   returned quietly to his desk.

In due time he was astonished to find
himself indicted for killing 90 thousand,
for neither he nor the killers he nurtured
were responsible for what had been ordered.

*Between June 1941 and July 1942, Otto Ohlendorf was in charge of *Einsatzgruppe* (Task Force) D, which was responsible for liquidating over 90,000 Jews in the Ukraine; afterwards he became a bureaucrat in Berlin. He was hanged after trial at Nuremberg on 8 June, 1951.

Desk Murderer*

Not abnormally antisemitic,
nor, apparently, sadistic;
who personally killed none,
was diligent to a fault:
not an obedient monster,
but a monster of obedience,
how explain Eichmann,
the Ultimate Forwarding Agent?

The fact is, that is *all* he was—
   yet, no less terrible
than Himmler's glint-spectacled evil,
or Heydrich's refined Nordic chill,
to Eichmann nothing attaches
   but functional guilt.

*The most efficient *Schreibtischtäter* ("desk murderer"), subordinate to Himmler and Heydrich, of the Final Solution: in his defence on trial in Jerusalem he protested that he was guilty only of obedience, which is a virtue. He was hanged on 31 March, 1962. "He *merely*, to put the matter colloquially, *never realized what he was doing.*" (Hannah Arendt, *Eichmann in Jerusalem*, 2nd ed., 1965).

Baldur von Schirach,
The Poet as War Criminal

("We wish to give meaning to our lives: the [Great] War spared
us for war": v Schirach's message to his generation)

Baptized in ironic travesty
after the Teutonic god of light,
destined to become *kitsch*-bard
to "a genius grazing the stars,"
and appointed as Misleader of Youth
whom in his verses he drugged
with images of struggle and death
exalted, to fall at the front
for Mozart and Germany,
Schirach seems the Nazi ironically
suited to govern cultured Vienna,
which he affirmed only music could conquer—
yet himself became tainted overseer
of its essential Jews' removal*:
approving this rather in principle
than SS practice, his queasy murmurs
set him stumbling from the Führer's grace . . .

Later, at Nuremberg he bemoaned
how falling in love with Hitler
had seduced him into complicity
with murder, as though he had rhymed
of no other death than his own.[†]

Entfernung, a typical euphemism for "extermination."
[†] "Not the adversary's death, but one's own death, was the burden of
Schirach's intoxicated utterances, and with him—and long before
him—one of the major themes of the younger generation" (Joachim C.
Fest, *The Face of the Third Reich*, 1970, 234). At Nuremberg he received 20
years' imprisonment for "polluting the minds of children, establishing the
Hitler Youth as a source of replacement for the Nazi Party, participating in

The Unrepentant Alois Brunner

Almost refreshing is the want of remorse
in the odious candour of Alois Brunner,*
killer by conviction, not compulsion:
"I regret nothing and would do it again."

No devious pleas, rationalizations
or craven bid for equal victimhood:
"I regret nothing and would do it again"—
in a forest of words his testimony
burns through and ignites the rest.

*Brunner (1912-) was Eichmann's right-hand man and a principal enforcer
of the Final Solution in France. Condemned there to death *in absentia* in
1954, he has since enjoyed government protection in Syria.

Gustav the Gleaner*

When at last the blitz battered his door
he wandered the grounds of the *Villa Hügel*,
scavenging shards of shell and shrapnel,
basketed windfalls, homing fruit of his war.

*Gustav Krupp von Bohlen and Halbach (1870-1950), the munitions king
who became an ardent Nazi convert, escaped trial as a war criminal
because of senility.

Enigmas

It is said they were tender fathers—
Goebbels, Bormann, Heydrich, Himmler—
like the best of ordinary men,
and Hitler himself, unchilded
but fatherly to those about him,
little secretaries, cooks, chauffeurs:
who all felt it homely at the Berghof
and found it beyond them to believe
their *Führer* knew what enormities
were done in his name.
                    Hard indeed it is
to detect the monsters among us—
harder, gratefully, to grasp what remorseful
fine beings their stainless children could become.

Inside Albert Speer*

(The Nazi "Faust")

Charmed by the dream Hitler offered,
Speer served him like a sleepwalker,
became his war's indispensable architect;
in Nuremberg's dock he stirred awake,
acknowledged just enough of the truth
to escape sharing premature death
with the slaves his factories devoured
and the Berlin Jews he drove from their homes—
then struggled through his life's long remnant
to translate what his conscience would say:
that, although aware, he looked away . . .

40

*Speer was both Hitler's favoured architect and Minister of Armaments and War Production. He received 20 years' imprisonment at Nuremberg, largely for exploiting slave labour, whereas Fritz Sauckel, who directly administered the forced labour policy, was hanged. However, Speer stood out among the accused in accepting "collective guilt" for the Nazis' extermination policy, but in *Inside the Third Reich*, compiled in Spandau Prison, he withheld full confession of what he had known until, near the end of his life, he capitulated under the persistent questioning of Gitta Sereny (see her *Albert Speer: His Struggle with Truth*, 1995). Dan Van Der Nat later, in *The Good Nazi*, (1997), proved Speer was responsible for having 75,000 Berlin Jews evicted from their homes.

Speer admitted to *Billigung*, "connivance through looking away" (Van Der Nat, p. 356). Hugh Trevor-Roper finds Speer "because of [his] moral blindness, 'the real criminal of Nazi Germany'" 'Hitler Revisited,' *Encounter* December 1988; the quotation within the quotation is from T-R's *The Last Days of Hitler* (1947).

Ribbentrop's Emptiness

(*Memoirs*, 1946)

Even as, amazed, he awaited execution
for complicity in his master's crimes,
still prepared, though about to die,
to deceive and be deceived by a lie,
in his arid, self-serving recollections
Ribbentrop maintains Hitler's "great aim"
was to save Western civilization . . .

He achieves more plausible narration
in recalling himself when young
listening from a corner enraptured
to a loved piano-playing mother
who would die soon; or how he won
his father's gift of a violin
that relieved his life's harsher chapters,

whether in the log cabins of Canada
or fearing the Slavic hordes of Russia:
burnished cameos of the life he lost.

The Marlows*

A redemptive few craved self-understanding,
felt bound through their life's remnant
to deathward monologue—

of what they had failed to foresee
in the smashed panes of *Kristallnacht*,
picked at their unassuageable guilt—

such were Speer and Münch,
Marlows to the Kurtz
Hitler and Mengele meant:

voices, minds they had not withstood—
"the fascination of the abomination."

*This poem alludes, in the characters of Marlow and Kurtz, and the final
quoted sentence, to Joseph Conrad's *Heart of Darkness*. Both Speer and
Münch declared their overwhelming admiration for Hitler and Mengele
respectively; Münch said, of Mengele, "I found his mind irresistible."
After the War, both lived out their lives driven by a need for
self-understanding (see G Sereny, *Speer: His Struggle with Truth* (1995), and
The German Trauma (2000)).

III

FOLLOWERS, BYSTANDERS,

RESISTERS, SUFFERERS

These people simply fail to recognize
The Devil, standing before their very eyes.
GOETHE, Faust

When the masses were shouting "Heil," what could
the individual person do? You went along. We were the
followers. That's how it was.
ERNA KRANZ
an "ordinary German"

Yet evil, as ruler, is of supreme importance; it is the
one condition of selfless good.
JACOB BURCKHARDT
Force and Freedom

Führer Faith

("If only the *Führer* knew . . ."*
  common saying)

Many made him a god
to answer their need,
blessed him for whatever was good,
but could not believe he knew
of the sins done in his name—
thus, humanly unaware
of every fallen sparrow,
he dwelt on a mountain top immune
from responsibility and blame.

*Wenn der Führer das nur Wusste . . .

Hitler Youth

How chill-clean they seem,
brown shirted, in step,
their Nation's classless blood—
the innately idealistic young, imbued
with perverted juvenile rectitude:
at ten, childhood cancelled, they began
their apprenticeship to War—
marched to fifes, drums and fanfares,
out of the mists of racial myth,
in a train of Germanic heroes,
Hitler foremost in a live drama,
their indoctrinated saga—
"You are nothing, the *Volk* is all."*

*Du bist nichts, Dein Volk ist alles.

45

Professor NSDAP*

(Ernst Jünger: "High treason of the spirit")

Booted, uniformed professors
were hot to acclaim New Life
in the beerhall savage, Adolf,
the Man with a Mouth,
avatar of The Risen People . . .

Men of idea and principle
eager for self-betrayal
in what they wrote and taught—
like Him who despised them, believing
words could mean all or nothing.

*The title adopts the caption to a photograph of a National Socialist college
lecturer by the Swiss photographer August Sander. NSDAP:
NationalsozialisticheDeutscheArbeiterpartei, the Nazi Party. "the Man with a
Mouth" (*Sprachmensch*): Hitler was so called by Anton Drexler, leader of
the German Workers' Party, upon his emergence in 1919.
For the poem's theme, see Viktor Klemperer, *I Shall Bear Witness*: "the
intelligentsia and scholars prostitute themselves" (p. 237), and Gordon A
Craig, *The Germans*: "4000 university teachers lost their positions after the
collapse of National Socialism in 1945." Many soon recovered them.

Heidegger in '33

Martin Heidegger, whom Being
deathwardly perturbed,
lapsed infamously when Time
was most real.Addressed
Hitler's brown-booted New Men
and authorized all they knew—

46

Earth and Blood
and *Deutsches Volk*:
withdrawing soon to the Black Forest
of *dasein**, made philosophical gain,
but involuntarily proved, in 33,
authentic choice between wood and tree.

* *"being-there"*— *dasein* is that (modern) being for whom
his being is problematic.

The German Christians*

(Deutsche Christen)

They sought to build a church of the brownshirt,
      a temple of the *Volkisch* spirit,
      whose good shepherd was Hitler,
      its flock storm troopers of the soul
      whose covenant War would seal—
      booted, riding-breeched pastors,
      führers of a "manly" church,
      every soldier's brothers:

Yet their mimicry of Nazi hardness and hate
was bound to fall short— not even an Aryan Jesus
could rule or save the one true Church of State.

*See Doris L Bergen, *Twisted Cross*: the German Christian Movement in the
Third Reich, 1996.

47

Avoiding Wagner

Wagner, who made magnificent music,
was rabidly antisemitic;
Herbert von Karajan,* who magnificently
conducted it, was twice a Nazi . . .
Should we, therefore, shun their art,
or, music and man being distinct—
though neither himself believed that—
bravo one, deplore the other?

None but the injured can forgive.
One gesture remains: to avoid.

*Herbert von Karajan "joined the Nazi Party not once, but twice" (Peter
Gay, *My German Question*, 1998). After the War, the opportunistic von
Karajan became the admired conductor of the Berlin Philharmonic.

Reading History During the Anschluss*

The afternoon of March 11, 1938. The Hall of Columns, the
Austrian Chancellery. The *Anschluss* imminent, all is bustle and
speculation, but with an underlying despair of salvation—as one
Cabinet member clearly understands, for he is noted in a corner,
finishing Burckhardt's *The Civilisation of the Renaissance in Italy*.
His name and reason for reading that history are not recorded,
but it may be surmised that he is an individual who sees through
and beyond the present moment.

Does he reflect that his doomed Vienna had, like Florence,
lately been a "scene of the richest development of human
individuality"?

Perhaps his copy would reveal that he had marked this
sentence: "In face of this centralized authority, all legal opposition
within the borders of the State was futile" (substituting "is" for

"was"). What then? What part would the reader play after the fact? Probably one such as Burckhardt discerns in the despotic Renaissance states: "Each individual protested inwardly against despotism but was disposed to make tolerable or profitable terms with it rather than to combine with others for its destruction."

In Austria, in 1938, few individuals could or would "combine" —though soon some would resist, "illegally." Let us imagine these included the reader in the corner. Forsaking stoical resignation for action, he thus became his own and his country's historian.

*Anschluss: the joining of Germany and Austria, forced by Hitler in 1938. The source for this prose is Gordon Brooke-Shepherd's *Anschluss: the Rape of Austria* (1963), concluding which he points out that, in the years under German hegemony, Austrians emerged from "confused ideas of nationhood . . . to find their own roots in the modern world." The shaping of the anecdote derives from the idea that historians *make* history. An even more striking historical parallel is the "Melian debate" in Thucydides' *The Peloponnesian War* (5th century BC.).

"Ordinary" Guilt*

However disgusted or compassionate,
few ordinary Germans could do
much to relieve the pariah Jew—
a few grams of forbidden coffee,
a scrap of rationed fish or meat,
illicit tobacco or a cigarette,
 dissenting words murmured
 where none could overhear,
a friendly visit by curfewed night:
to attempt more would gamble the fate
of your near and dear, children above all,
against an unsung moral martyrdom,
lost in the camps, your protest unheard:
it was thus "decent Germans" must choose.

*This poem was prompted chiefly by reading Viktor Klemperer's *I Shall Bear Witness*, who writes "There is no doubt that the people feel the persecution of the Jews to be a sin" (p. 438). Klemperer, a Jew with an "Aryan" wife, escaped the ultimate Jewish fate.

Brother Hitler in Black and White

Thomas Mann acknowledged him as "brother"*—
the indolent drop out and lay about,
bohemian would-be artist, buoyed
by radical contempt for prosaic life—
slighted genius in wait for his moment—

diagnosed in him art as "black magic"
that the *hopeful* artist, if he first can
overcome the aloof detachment
on which his ironic conscience reclines,
must as "white enchanter" confront.

*See Thomas Mann, 'Brother' (1938) in his *Order of the Day* (1942).

50

"Befehl ist Befehl"*

("Orders are Orders")

This meant in deep translation
utter abdication of conscience,
but even troubled, decent men
were kept, despite easy occasion,
from forswearing the oath to the Führer
his generals themselves had devised
and performing the necessary murder
of the master of rationalized slaughter:

> In revulsion from what he was
> they would themselves practise
> purely superior motive and act—
> and so did nothing.

*In 1758 the Wurtemmberg publisher, Karl Friedrich Moser, identified obedience as the "principal motive" of the German nation. Ulrich von Hassell, deploring the indecisiveness of generals opposed to Hitler's war policy, caustically comments, "Those generals who want to overthrow governments demand orders from these very governments before they will act!" "The oath:" devised, not by Hitler (who readily accepted it), but by Reichenau and Blomberg, the *Reichswehr* leadership, as the old Chancellor, Hindenburg, whom Hitler succeeded, lay dying (I Kershaw, *Hitler*, p. 525). Ironically, Hitler had himself provided a justificatory text for reluctant assassins in *Mein Kampf*, "especially when a people languishes under the tyranny of some oppressor genius" (Vol. 2, Chapt. IX). Prussian military law also laid down that orders with a criminal intent should not be obeyed. However, for evidence that unquestioning obedience to inhumane policy and orders did not only characterize the German military, see Nikolai Tolstoy, *Victims of Yalta* (1977).

Knowing: a Conundrum*

You did not know
because you did not ask;
you did not ask
because you knew . . .

*"I did not want to know" (Albert Speer); ". . . .closing our eyes to it, we
did not 'consciously' know what it was" (Anne Marie Kempf, Speer's
secretary); "It is possible to live in a twilight between knowing and not
knowing" (W A Visser t'Hooft, *Memoirs*, 1973).

"Burn Me Too!"

(Letter to Goebbels, 1934)

May these words serve as upright epitaph
    for novelist Oskar Maria Graf.*

*Graf, a humanitarian revolutionary, went into exile, first in
Czechoslovakia, and from 1938, like Mann, in the United States. The
book-burning, orchestrated by Goebbels, took place in several university
towns, including Berlin, 10 May 1933.

Fritz Gerlich, Journalist

(Murdered in Dachau, on the Night
of the Long Knives, 30 June 1934)

Was it a calculating cruel irony
that the Gestapo returned to his widow
Fritz Gerlich's blood-spattered spectacles,
steel-rimmed symbol of a vision
that had stung with the unavailing word?

Such voices are too little remembered:
no plaque marks the site where he
scrutinized the proofs of *Der Gerade Weg**;
an intense lamp glints on his glasses,
brownshirts beat and bawl in the street.

*("The Straight Way"), a critical conservative
paper Gerlich edited for a decade.

A Patriot's Dilemma

(from the Diaries of Ulrich
von Hassell, August 1939)

"The real Germany" seemed a sunny Sunday
morning in Tübingen, bells proclaiming
the hymn, "Wake up, a voice is calling us":
across the old market square, by the Rathaus,
families peacefully stream chapel-wards;
others climb to the castle above the Neckar:
behind this picture, mocking bells and worship,
spread the camps crammed with the excluded,
while soon over the frontier such towns in Poland

will be blown apart, and obedient young Germans
hunt down their neighbours best . . .
                              How prevent this,
why speak out when swift, cruel silencing
will instantly cancel all one is,
thrust shame and disgust against a wall?

The Incredible SS Man

Truth never hurts the teller
                    ROBERT BROWNING

Kurt Gerstein, deliverer of Zyklon B,
incredibly assumed evil's uniform
that he might become God's spy*—
and daringly sought to sabotage
the deadly canisters in his charge.

"In tears and with a breaking voice"
he testified of slaughter he had witnessed
to a Swedish diplomat who did his hopeless best—
but few believed Gerstein's rare resistance
for he approached in demonic dress . . .

At war's end, arrested for his black disguise,
he killed himself in Cherche Midi—
or fell victim to French avengers—
the extreme conscience of his *Volk*
consumed by the burning truth he wore.

*God's Spy: see Rolf Hochhuth, *The Representative*, p. 63. Gerstein almost
certainly killed himself in Cherche Midi, a Paris prison, 23 July 1945;
Hochhuth, however, thinks it likely that he was among "the still
uncounted Germans and Frenchmen who were murdered without trial in

France after the liberation of 1944" (p. 275). See also Saul Friedländer, Kurt *Gerstein:_the Ambiguity of Good*, 1969.

Geschwister-Scholl*

Scarcely a movement, only a few
of deep faith and shaming decency
who renounced the secure little house
to fire paper darts of light
at the black iron walls of state:
Hans and Sophie, *Geschwister-Scholl*,
twofold heart of the White Rose,
found their truth of being in speech
that would not be stilled until,
in joyous martyrdom Himmler sought
too late to deny them, they bathed
in Christ's wounds, became symbol
like Him of reckless humanity.

* Brother-and-sister Scholl, Hans and Sophie, central to the small, mainly students' resistance group, *Weisse Rose* (The White Rose), in Munich; beheaded by the Gestapo, 22 February, 1943, aged 24 and 21. In a letter to a friend, 2 May, 1941, Hans asks, "Should one go off and build a little house with flowers outside the windows and a garden outside the door and extol and thank God and turn one's back on the world and its filth?" "Isn't seclusion a form of treachery, of desertion?. . . I'm weak and puny, but I want to do what is right" (*At the Heart of the_White Rose*, ed. Inge Jens, 1987, p. 112). The square fronting the main building of the University of Munich is named Geschwister-Scholl Platz.

Von Moltke of Kreisau*

Sire, grant us freedom of thought
SCHILLER, Don Carlos

He could, he said have drunk tea
in his warm room, and done nothing,
like many who were decently disturbed:
instead, he worked within to mitigate—
and inspired, centred on his old estate,
a circle to formulate a rational
future freedom of citizens obedient
to humane conscience, above the Total State.

Although he took part in no plot,
it was plain they must murder him
solely for what he thought . . .

*Helmut James Graf von Moltke (1907-45) was the "Moving Spirit" of the
Kreisau Circle (so called by the Gestapo), centred upon his estate at
Kreisau, Silesia, now part of Poland; its members discussed those
principles that should guide a post-Nazi Germany. Although he had
already been imprisoned for six months before the 20th July, 1944, attempt
on Hitler's life, he was killed in its aftermath. Vera Lips (*Savage Symphony*,
1938) records that the words from Schiller's *Don Carlos* were "simply
omitted" from a Hamburg production, but that the audience applauded at
the appropriate place. Associated with the Circle was the courageous
defence lawyer, Carl Langbehn, subject of the next poem.

Supping with Himmler (1941)

(Carl Langbehn, Counsel for the Defence, 1901–44)

Dining with the *Reichsführer S S*,
he broached the impropriety
of killing men without due process
and mailing them to their wives in ashes.

A surprised Himmler undertook to enquire
and, should it prove true,
to liquidate the culprits—
only for Langbehn to argue
that, too, was a matter for the law:

How injudiciously judicious he was—
still, they let him plead two years more.

Tapir, a Surrogate Victim*

Among those few characters who redeem,
      in Vera Lips' *Savage Symphony*,
is one named Tapir, her Boxer dog;
he never learned to utter Heil Hitler!
and his *Weltanschauung* was simple—
a bone, a chewed ball, a straw-lined kennel:
he never understood why those he loved,
squeezed into exile, vanished from his world—
though they found him a carefully chosen master
among remote, bounding rural delights,
others tracked him down, with a poisoned treat,
and left beneath his body a note of hate—
that he was murdered as surrogate for Lips,

the Professor who "would not yield to Hitler."

Although in the German Shepherd-fond
Führer's state, of myriad human martyrdoms,
animals like Tapir have no monument,
they belong with the choiceless innocents,
worthy of remembrance with all who loved,
were loved, but could not be saved by laws,
prayers—or love, to be lamented
with every trusting creature, even Hitler's own.

*See Vera Lips, *Savage Symphony*, a Personal Record of the Third Reich,
NY, 1938. It was reported that a woman claimed her dog had learned to
say "Heil Hitler!"

Mock Execution of a French Résistant (1944)*

At the sun-filled angle of two walls,
head slightly bowed,
eyes shadowed,
forehead high, white,
he seems smiling:
hands out of sight
pinned back, chest narrow,
bared, he waits at ease.

Ranked between us and him,
the German firing squad takes aim,
awaits its officer's word,
who stands, neck open for the heat,
fists at belted waist,
seems weighing his powered moment
to remove the other from the sun.

The word "Fire!" never came:
they only meant to make him speak,
but whether he did so or not
he would disappear in a camp,
nothing left but this snapshot
in a dead German officer's pocket,
grinning on in careless undress
at the murderous charade.

The Illustrated London News, "Victory 45" Number, May 1995

Schindler's Neglected Counterpart: The Other Göring

Womanizer, gourmand of good life,
sharer of an omnipotent name,
Albert was a privileged candidate
for loot in the Nazi robber-state:
yet his humanity transcended blood—
which, nevertheless, he riskily
exploited, tapped brother Hermann's
vestigial conscience, goaded his shifty
opportunism into penning edicts
that saved marked Jews in Vienna and Prague,
snatched Czech colleagues even from Heydrich;
among those for whom he intervened
was Franz Léhar who, though the Führer
loved his *Merry Widow*, was haplessly
blessed with a Jewish wife . . .

Yet Albert was no hero after the War,
condemned to wear until death
an irredeemable name, like a yellow star.

In Memoriam Joseph Weinheber
"Poet Laureate" of "Ostmark"*

(committed suicide 1945)

Auden, who chanced to settle
in your village of Kirchstetten,
made, in passing, daily obeisance
to your garden-grave, reflecting
perhaps that certain poets fitted
rather to play viols on the green
may, confounding soil with blood,
their small world with the larger,
stumble into complicity with crimes
their words naively celebrate:
in slitting, at the last, your lying lyric
       you rejoined the few
       Auden knew, who
       keep truth's account.

*See W H Auden, "Joseph Weinheber," *Collected Poems*, 1976, p. 568. Hilde Spiel describes Weinheber as a National Socialist party member and "poeta laureatus of the Ostmark," while Austria was so called; "he lived to regret this decision and died atoning for it, by his own hand" (*Vienna's Golden Autumn*, 1987).

Ordinary Virtues*

1. Mother
Mrs Tenenbaum understood you cannot argue about making a gift of your life. A nurse, whose deportation was briefly deferred, she asked her daughter to hold her pass a moment while she went upstairs. There she swallowed a killing dose of luminal, which

left no room for discussion. With her three months' legacy of life, her mother's pass, the daughter knew love and happiness.

2. Daughter

It was one of those stifling summer's days when your every step is a weighty effort. When Pola turned the corner at last, her street was strangely quiet, strewn with pieces of clothing, here and there a burst, abandoned suitcase, some pots and pans. A dead man sprawled across the sidewalk not far from her home, his head bleeding into the gutter, a hand still clutching a cardboard valise held together with string. She rushed up to the tiny room they shared with an old couple. It was deserted and disordered. She did not hesitate, but ran—and ran. Meeting her boyfriend, she made him balance her on his bike, or she'd be too late. Now, as always, he asked no question, but pedalled her off in the heavy heat, towards the station. The straggling column, harried by shouts of Schnell! Schnell!, driven by rifle butts, was almost there when they caught up. Pola had him pedal slowly past until, seeing her mother, she jumped off with a goodbye and ran to seize her stumbling mother's arm. Together they reached the station, entered the same wagon, and together they died in Treblinka.

3. Sister

The little girl yearned, before she died, to see something green. Her sister, chancing her life, crept beneath the ghetto wall. She returned, bearing a leaf from the forbidden Aryan park. Sucking her thumb and smiling at the leaf in a glass, the little girl died.

*1 and 2 are narrated in Hanna Kroll and Marek Edelman, *Shielding the Flame*, N.Y. 1977; 3 is a story from the Warsaw Ghetto.

Two Fathers*

(The Warsaw Ghetto, 1942)

"Have you no pity?"
"I must have your kid,
or they will take mine;
call me, if you like,
a wild beast. Perhaps I am."

My children or yours,
yours or mine, pity
a weak figment:
a plea we can comprehend,
a choice we dare not imagine.

*An incident recounted in Lucy S Davidowicz, *The War Against the Jews,
1939-45*, p. 304. Both fathers are Jews, the one with power, albeit limited, a
ghetto policeman expected to fulfil his quota of victims for the transports
to the camps.

"Kanada" at Auschwitz

After the Jews had been forwarded from life,
their last possessions were sorted and stored
in *"Kanada,"* that infinitely remote
bountiful land.* Nothing was too trivial
for that cut-price emporium where
trusty prisoners and their guards bartered
clothes, shoes, glasses, precious toothbrushes:
in that hell a heaven, where flowed
a ceaseless spring of goods on sale
priced in despised, disposable lives.

Himmler's Auschwitz Visit

A Survivor Remembers

The day Heinrich Himmler came visiting,
Yankel Meisel was some tunic buttons short,
so they dragged him out of line
and beat him to death: he wouldn't die easy,
but set up a wail like broken bagpipes . . .

Luckily, it stopped the very minute
Himmler arrived, greeted by our orchestra
with the Triumph March from *Aida*:
as, smiling, Himmler reviewed us,
we hoped he would improve our lives.

Selektion

I heard them call out my name,
but it was another, not me, they meant:
relieved, I survived beyond shame.

"The Last One"*

As, merely alive,
they stood by,
subdued to survive,
they heard him cry,
"Comrades, I am the last one!"
That he could freely die
took root as shameful memory
in those reduced to live on.

*See Primo Levi, *Survival in Auschwitz*, the chapter entitled "The Last
One:" the words are those spoken by a man, about to be hanged before the
camp's inmates, for having supported the revolt of the *Sonderkommando*
(Jews designated for special work) in Birkenau.

Illustrations

Turning pages, you meet them again
enclosed in atrocious chronicles,
that frieze of wrenching photographs:
a quaking boy raises hands before
the gun, his thin satchel for the journey,
outsize cap into which he will not grow;
a trio of short-trousered boys hasten,
hands clutched, towards the Birkenau
gas chamber, the biggest, perhaps ten,
protective in the middle; another boy
peers from a cattle car en route
for Theresianstadt, black holes for eyes;
the shivering women, desperate to end it,
queue naked for the slaughter pit;
a soldier, with rifle raised,
on a bare, open plain, caught

in the instant of shooting
a Jewish mother, her child clasped
in vain protection to her chest
(one bullet will do for both);
ashes from the Inferno by chance
coalesced, a few nameless shapes
endlessly beyond intervening touch.

Goethe at Buchenwald

When they felled the forest,
voiding the name of Buchenwald,
the Nazis, mindful of *Kultur*,
preserved the Oak of Goethe
under their Nature Protection Act:
there, reclining beside Eckermann
upon a green hill, Goethe mused
"Here one feels great and free."

American bombs ignited the tree,
but in a billet of its wood he saved
a camp inmate carved a human face—
hoping, somehow, to redeem that place?

Schiller's Melted Statue

Not even converting the melted metal
of joyous Schiller to ammunition
could demolish that "mighty line"
Marquis Posa ventures to the King:
"Sire, give us freedom of thought."*

*See note on Von Moltke of Kreisau, p. 56.

Rilke at Dachau

"Behind the innocent trees
    old Fate is slowly forming
    her taciturn face."*

With the breaking twentieth century
often Rilke summered there,
but not even he could intuit
the chill shadow encroaching
upon that artists' colony of
"innocent trees."
                    Yet he was,
in romantic lyrical fashion,
obsessed with how to die—
whether calmly or in thrashing rage
would denote how one had lived:
not stripped, shaven, herded
to a last gasp of gas or shot in the nape.

Hinter den schuldlosen Barmen, Rilke August 1913 (trans. JB Leishman)

DP

(Displaced Person*)

Your home was stolen or burned,
your possessions—books keepsakes
icons photographs—seized or destroyed,
your land churned to dust,
your dear ones killed before you:
     uprooted,
you rotted almost to death,
in camps dug outs cellars
of smashed buildings;
endlessly you trudged to survive
from one oppression to another:
     at the end of it all,
       human rubble,
       you awaited disposal.

*At the end of the war, millions of "displaced persons" in Europe were
thought of, less in terms of that euphemism than as a plague of rats or
locusts, even human scum. See M Marrus, *The Unwanted: European Refugees
in the Twentieth Century* (1985), M. Eksteins, *Walking Until Daybreak* (1999).

Reflecting Upon Samuel Drix's 'Witness'

Utterly outside that experience, one cannot judge Dr Samuel Drix's *Witness*, his memoir of Holocaust survival, except in one aspect: for those who acted atrociously, he has only the word "beast." Primarily, this means an animal other than a human being, but secondly, "a brutal person," which may mean simply cruel, or animal-like. The common simile is not his but originates somewhere in the human mind that seeks to repudiate what it is capable of. Those immune from or who have mastered instinctive cruelty would mistakenly divorce not only themselves but the human race from those who act cruelly, without conscience.

Yet Drix is one who shows how numerous they were—not only the master torturers, murderers and sadists, but also their collaborators, driven by ethnic hatred or the desire to survive or prosper by betraying others. Drix, towards the end, forgetting his bestial analogies, writes, "After all I had seen, I had lost my idealism about the human race . . . I did not want to sacrifice and postpone my own needs for the sake of this humanity." Nevertheless, he would again practise as a doctor and serve that "humanity."

Later, he would bear witness against certain murderers, only to see most "punished" with derisory sentences. Although the worst, Friedrich Heinen, who killed for sport hundreds who unluckily met his eyes, his "kind blue eyes," was largely through Drix's evidence, over 20 years after the War's end, sentenced to life imprisonment. What had Heinen done, how had he lived during those post war years?

Perhaps as an "ordinary" human being, his licence to kill having been withdrawn. How many among us would eagerly grasp that licence if another such as Hitler and his henchmen were to offer it? We cannot know whom we live among; our hope is to live and die in ignorance and illusion, among the caged, unrecognized ones.

The Righteous Dutch*

Unequivocal as their landscape,
a few accepted the flat imperative
to shield the hunted stranger:
the rest prudently refrained— yet
shunned, rebuked or betrayed those
who chanced *their* indifferent lives.

*". . . These are righteous Gentiles," celebrated by Yad Vashem (The Israeli
War Memorial Authority) in its "Avenue of the Righteous" in Jerusalem.

"Not a Bird"*

It was no bird, but a baby in flight
that the hunter soon brought down,
then shot the maddened mother;
this, of every atrocity she witnessed
returned most often in her dreams,
the slaughter of the incontestably innocent.

Among those she saved in hiding
what meant most was that one
inside the horror gave birth.

*From Irene Gut Opdyke, *In My Hands, Memories of a
Holocaust Rescuer*, 1999.

69

Efforts at Remembrance

(1998)

They come from all over in the March of the Living, yearning to remember and reach their obliterated forebears, whether crouching at the domed Mound of Ashes or in barracks and "bath houses" that reek of fear and despair beyond all empathy. They light small candles in those places and at the lips of the ovens. These are their wordless poems. Most weep—or, stone faced, cannot. One fingers the barbed wire, nearly hard enough to bleed; an abundant-haired girl, staring at the glassed-in locks and braids—still as their owners plaited them—absently winds her own, teasing it with small jerks as if to pull it clear of her scalp. Many merely sit, gaze about them, fighting to feel enough. "The day we came," says one, "was wet and grey." She felt confined. "Now the sky's blue and I feel freer." "I cannot," confesses another, "pray to God here—where was He then?"

A survivor asks, "But where was Man?"

The Question

Lies and lethargies police the world
In its periods of peace. What pain taught
is soon forgotten.

WH AUDEN, *The Age of Anxiety*

Whoever thinks should ask, now and for the future,
What might I have been under Hitler?
One who dared from lectern, pulpit or crowd
cry Murder! and was dragged to silence
by thugs in brown? Or a covert dissenter
who raised a wooden arm in official greeting?
Or one who by degrees trimmed to the worst
and never knew, looking back, where you fell?

Most, as ever, apathetic or gripped by fear,
accepted, as they would, whoever ruled.
Most guilty were not the crass criminals,
ideologues of hate, even bullies or sadists,
but the cool prostitutes of intellect—
writers, scholars, philosophers, professors
who, to keep position or clutch power,
sold their reason and their moral being . . .

To think one would have stood with the best above these
is to claim self-knowledge beyond Socrates.

ACKNOWLEDGEMENTS

I am especially grateful for a Creation Grant from the New Brunswick Department of Economic Development, Tourism and Culture, administered by the province's Arts Board; it greatly facilitated the necessary research for this work.

Once again, I have greatly benefited from Peter Sanger's stimulating and unsparing responses to the penultimate typescript; those prompted, I hope, some improvements.

Two poems, "Heidegger in '33" and "Mock Execution of a French Résistant" are reprinted from earlier volumes, *Bagdad is Everywhere* and *Loves*.